T0395632

WHAT DOES THE SECRET SERVICE DO?

★★★ DANIELLE HAYNES

PowerKiDS press™

Published in 2026 by The Rosen Publishing Group, Inc.
2544 Clinton Street, Buffalo, NY 14224

First Edition

Editor: Dwayne Hicks
Book Design: Rachel Rising

Photo Credits: Cover, Sharomka/Shutterstock.com; Cover, pp. 5, 9, 14, 16, 21 https://en.m.wikipedia.org/wiki/File:USSS_New_Star.svg; Cover, pp. 1, 3-24 Madan Designer/Shutterstock.com; Cover, pp. 1, 3-24 Art Posting/Shutterstock.com; p. 4 Joseph Sohm/Shutterstock.com; p. 5 Andrew Leyden/Shutterstock.com; p. 7 https://commons.wikimedia.org/wiki/File:Assassination_attempt_on_Jackson_(cropped).jpg; p. 8 Ian Peter Morton/Shutterstock.com; p. 9 Harris & Ewing, photographer. Checking over confiscated counterfeit currency at the Secret Service Div. ofthe Treasury, 10/38. [October] Photograph. Retrieved from the Library of Congress, <www.loc.gov/item/2016874188/>.; p. 10 BreizhAtao/Shutterstock.com; p. 11 https://commons.wikimedia.org/wiki/File:Kristi_Noem_with_Mike_Johnson_in_2025.jpg; p. 11 https://commons.wikimedia.org/wiki/File:Sean_Curran_official_portrait.jpg; p. 13 https://commons.wikimedia.org/wiki/File:Secret_Service_agents_protecting_President_Obama_and_First_Lady_Michelle_Obama.png; p. 15 https://commons.wikimedia.org/wiki/File:President_Ronald_Reagan_moments_before_he_was_shot_in_an_assassination_attempt_1981.jpg; p. 17 Aaron of L.A. Photography/Shutterstock.com; p. 18 New Africa/Shutterstock.com; p. 19 RomanR/Shutterstock.com; p. 20 DimaBerlin/Shutterstock.com; p. 21 Robert Przybysz/Shutterstock.com.

Cataloging-in-Publication Data

Names: Haynes, Danielle.
Title: What does the Secret Service do? / Danielle Haynes.
Description: Buffalo, New York : PowerKids Press, 2026. | Series: U.S. government agencies | Includes glossary and index.
Identifiers: ISBN 9781499453201 (pbk.) | ISBN 9781499453218 (library bound) | ISBN 9781499453225 (ebook)
Subjects: LCSH: United States. Secret Service–Juvenile literature. | Secret service–United States–Juvenile literature. | Law enforcement–United States–Juvenile literature.
Classification: LCC HV8144.S43 H38 2026 | DDC 363.28'30973–dc23

Manufactured in the United States of America

CPSIA Compliance Information: Batch #CSPK26. For Further Information contact Rosen Publishing at 1-800-237-9932.

Find us on

CONTENTS

WHAT IS THE SECRET SERVICE?

Have you ever noticed the security officials who follow around the president, vice president, and members of their families? Sometimes they're dressed in black suits, wearing sunglasses. Sometimes they look more like **law enforcement officers**, with bulletproof vests and large guns.

These guards are member of the U.S. Secret Service. They're one of the United States's oldest law enforcement agencies. Their main job is to keep the president and other important government officials safe. But they do more than just that. Did you know the Secret Service was first formed to stop the use of **counterfeit** money? Let's learn more about this important government agency!

AGENCY INSIGHTS

The U.S. Secret Service has more than 6,500 people as special agents, officers, and support workers.

This Secret Service officer guards the president's car as they return to the White House.

RESTRICTED AREA
DO NOT ENTER

5

PROTECTING THE PRESIDENT

The Secret Service was formed in 1865, but even before then, the U.S. president needed protection. In the early days of the United States, bodyguards kept the president and White House safe.

Sometimes, the Army protected the president, and sometimes local police did when they traveled. For the most part, though, presidents went unprotected compared to what happens today. For example, President Thomas Jefferson walked unguarded to his own **inauguration** in 1801. Martin Van Buren, who was president from 1837 to 1841, liked to walk to church alone. The first attempt to **assassinate** a U.S. president came on January 30, 1835, when a man tried to shoot Andrew Jackson, but missed.

Would-be assassin Richard Lawrence, pictured at the right holding a gun, takes aim at President Andrew Jackson, the taller figure of the two men in the center. Jackson was said to have raised his cane to strike Lawrence in response to the gunfire.

BIRTH OF THE SECRET SERVICE

The Secret Service was created on July 5, 1865, less than three months after actor John Wilkes Booth assassinated President Abraham Lincoln at Ford's Theatre. However, the agency wasn't established to keep presidents safe at first.

At the time, counterfeit money was a huge problem. More than one-third of all paper currency in the United States was fake. The U.S. Treasury Department established the Secret Service to **investigate** and fight counterfeiting. It took the assassinations of two more presidents—Andrew Garfield in 1881 and William McKinley in 1901—for the Secret Service to make presidential security its main job.

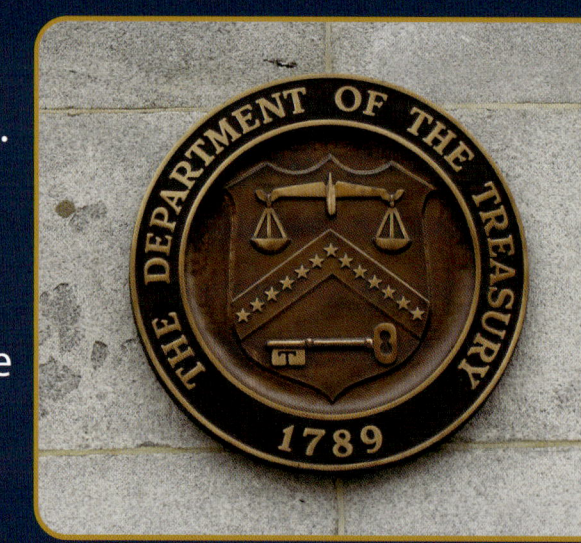

AGENCY INSIGHTS

In November 1864, the Washington, D.C., police created the first force to guard the president. The officer who was supposed to be watching President Lincoln on the night of his death in April 1865 was next door to Ford's Theatre and not at his post.

A Secret Service worker reviews **confiscated** counterfeit currency in 1938.

9

HOMELAND SECURITY

Though the Secret Service originally began as part of the Treasury Department, the agency's purpose shifted more toward security in the 20th century. Starting in 2003, the Secret Service became part of the Department of Homeland Security (DHS). The DHS is one of 15 **cabinet**-level departments that operate under the president of the United States. The heads of these departments are known as secretaries, which are appointed by the president and approved by the U.S. Senate.

In early 2025, President Donald Trump named Kristi Noem as DHS secretary and Sean Curran as director of the Secret Service. The Secret Service director answers to the DHS secretary.

Kristi Noem (left) served in the U.S. House of Representatives before becoming DHS secretary. Sean Curran (right) had worked for the Secret Service since 2001 before being named director.

WHO IS PROTECTED?

While many people know the Secret Service best for protecting the president, the agency protects many other people. They're called protectees. Among them are:

- vice president
- president-elect
- vice president-elect
- the immediate families of the president, vice president, president-elect, and vice president-elect
- former presidents and their **spouses**
- children of former presidents until the age of 16
- visiting **foreign** heads of state, their spouses, and other important foreign **dignitaries**
- major presidential and vice-presidential candidates and their spouses

- other people chosen by the president
- important national security events chosen by DHS

Former presidents may refuse Secret Service protection, and former first ladies lose their protection if they remarry. Members of Congress decide which presidential candidates can receive protection.

Several Secret Service agents walk with President Barack Obama and First Lady Michelle Obama during a 2017 parade.

TAKING A BULLET

Many people like to say that a Secret Service agent's job is to take a bullet for the president. That means they're willing to step in front of the president if they're being shot at. This is a very rare possibility, but it is part of the job. Certain Secret Service workers agree to sacrifice their lives to keep their protectees safe in dangerous situations.

One agent who did this very thing is Tim McCarthy. He put himself between a shooter and President Ronald Reagan during an attack in 1981. Reagan was seriously injured in the attack. McCarthy took one of the bullets in his chest. Luckily, both men survived.

AGENCY INSIGHTS

Washington, D.C., police officer Thomas Delahanty was also injured during the assassination attempt. Reagan's press secretary, James Brady, suffered brain damage and eventually died from his injuries in 2014.

Secret Service Agent Tim McCarthy (right) keeps an eye on President Ronald Reagan (left) shortly before the assassination attempt.

BEHIND THE SCENES

The most visible roles in the Secret Service are the special agents who accompany the president and other officials. But there are many other people often working behind the scenes.

Uniformed officers also attend events and venues where protectees will be. They monitor and keep these places safe. Many officers will be on hand to secure a **venue** even before a protectee gets there. Finally, there are civil service workers, people who do office work or investigate financial crimes, such as counterfeiting. Some of these people work at field offices across the United States, not just in the capital of Washington, D.C.

AGENCY INSIGHTS

The Secret Service has more than 150 field offices in the United States and in other countries. These are smaller offices separate from the headquarters.

Sometimes you might see uniformed Secret Service officers on roofs near an outdoor space where a protectee will be. They keep watch from afar.

17

COUNTERFEIT MONEY

Even though the Secret Service is now mostly known for protecting important government figures, it still does its original job—counterfeit investigations. With modern technology, fake currency is sometimes hard to detect. Luckily, the Secret Service has its own tools to root it out and track down the criminals making it. The agency is even able to stop credit card **fraud** and digital financial crimes.

This is an incredibly important job. The agency said it seized nearly $22 million in counterfeit bills in 2023. The Secret Service even advises the Treasury Department—and foreign governments—on the best currency designs to prevent counterfeiting.

U.S. currency has many safety features to prevent it from being counterfeited easily. The $100 bill, for instance, has a special strip running through the center of it.

A CAREER IN THE SECRET SERVICE

 Are you interested in working for the Secret Service one day? Luckily, there are many career paths you can take to join the agency. You might want to get a college degree in criminal justice or finance to help you track down and catch criminals.

 The Secret Service is entrusted with taking care of some of the highest government officials, so you must have a clean background. The agency wants to make sure you don't have a criminal history. There are also many training and **internship** programs for young people considering a career with the agency.

Many Secret Service workers must carry a gun to protect their charges. They must undergo training to use these guns safely.

GLOSSARY

assassinate: To kill someone, especially a public figure.

cabinet: A committee of government officials who help the president run the country.

confiscate: To take something away that is illegal or not allowed.

counterfeit: Something that's made to look like something else but is fake.

dignitary: A person who has a high rank or important position.

foreign: Something or someone that is from a country other than your own.

fraud: Telling lies in order to get something of value or the right to something.

inauguration: A ceremony in which a president is sworn into office.

internship: An educational or training program that gives experience for a career.

investigate: To examine and gather evidence about a crime.

law enforcement officer: A person who works for a government department that is formed with the purpose of making sure laws are followed.

spouse: A husband, wife, or significant other.

venue: A place where something happens.

FOR MORE INFORMATION

BOOKS

Banks, Rosie. *Currency*. Buffalo, NY: Gareth Stevens Publishing, 2024.

Lowell, Barbara. *Secret Service*. Mankato, MN: Black Rabbit Books, 2024.

WEBSITES

Kiddle: Assassination of Abraham Lincoln
www.kids.kiddle.co/Assassination_of_Abraham_Lincoln
Read more about the assassination of President Abraham Lincoln.

U.S. Secret Service
www.secretservice.gov
Learn more about the roles the Secret Service plays on the agency's official website.

INDEX